CRAYOLA
COLOR IN
NATURE

Mari Schuh

Lerner Publications ◆ Minneapolis

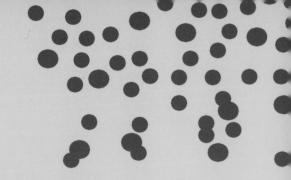

FOR FAIRMONT, THE CITY OF LAKES

Official Licensed Product
Lerner Publications Company
A division of Lerner Publishing Group, Inc.
241 First Avenue North
Minneapolis, MN 55401 USA

For reading levels and more information, look up this title at www.lernerbooks.com.

Main body text set in Billy Infant Regular 24/40.
Typeface provided by SparkyType.

Library of Congress Cataloging-in-Publication Data

Names: Schuh, Mari C., 1975– author.
Title: Color in nature / by Mari Schuh.
Other titles: Crayola color in nature
Description: Minneapolis : Lerner Publications, [2018] | Series: Crayola colorology | Audience: Ages 4–9. | Audience: K to grade 3. | Includes bibliographical references and index.
Identifiers: LCCN 2017027389 (ebook) | LCCN 2017021598 (print) | ISBN 9781512497748 (eb pdf) | ISBN 9781512466904 (lb : alk. paper) | ISBN 9781541511644 (pb : alk. paper)
Subjects: LCSH: Animals—Color—Juvenile literature. | Camouflage (Biology)—Juvenile literature. | Colo r—Juvenile literature.
Classification: LCC QL767 (print) | LCC QL767 .S37 2018 (ebook) | DDC 591.47/2—dc23

LC record available at https://lccn.loc.gov/2017021598

Manufactured in the United States of America
1-43081-32455-8/28/2017

TABLE OF CONTENTS

BRIGHT AND BEAUTIFUL

High in the sky and deep in the ocean, nature is full of color!

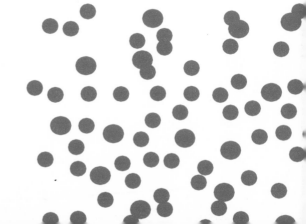

COLORS THAT HIDE

Do you see the lizards hiding in the hot desert?

They find rocks that match their skin color.

Many animals use color to hide from other animals.

A snowy owl hunts for food on the cold, snowy land. Its fluffy white feathers match the pure white snow.

Can you find the sneaky snake hiding in the rain forest?

A wild lion roams a grassland looking for food. The lion's tan fur helps it hide in the tall tan grass.

A butterfly rests on tree bark. The butterfly's dull colors blend in. Predators won't see it!

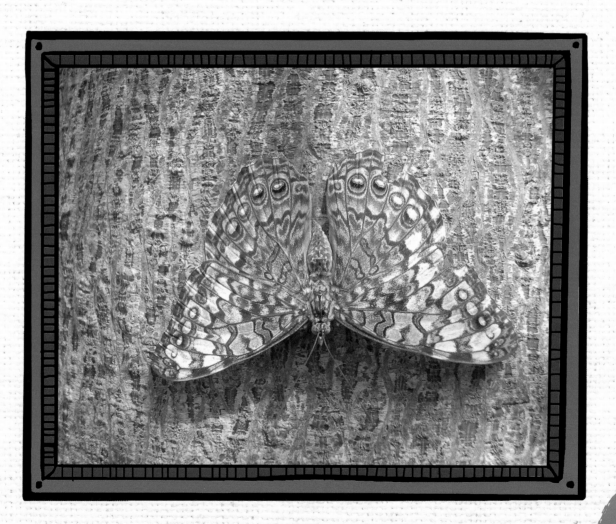

Dull colors help female birds hide. Hiding keeps the birds' eggs and young safe.

Which bird do you think is the female?

COLORS THAT WARN

The ladybug doesn't taste good to predators. Its red body warns birds and bugs to stay away.

A wasp's yellow body scares away predators. The wasp can sting!

Bright blue rings cover an octopus. Stay back!

The octopus has poison when it bites.

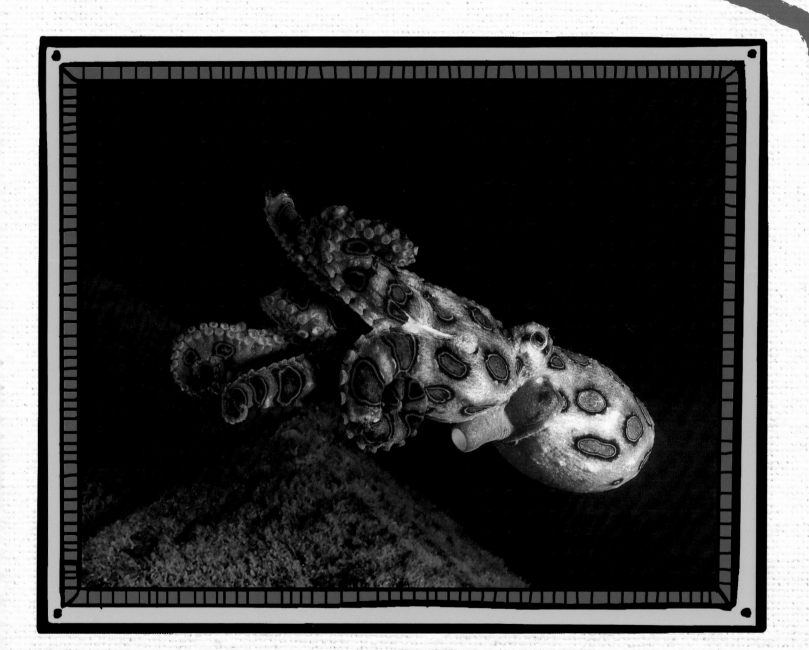

A skunk's black-and-white fur is easy to see. The colors warn others to stay far away.

The skunk can spray a stinky liquid!

Watch out!

A tree frog flashes its bright red eyes. The bright color surprises predators.

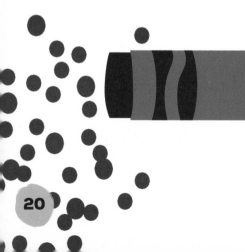

What other bright colors does this frog have?

COLORS THAT ATTRACT

Birds visit bright pink, yellow, and blue flowers.

The birds sip nectar from the flowers.

Look at these bold colors!

Male birds use their colorful feathers to get attention from females.

Big feathers and bright colors tell females that the males are healthy.

AMAZING COLORS

Amazing colors fill the night sky. So many beautiful colors are found in nature.

What colors do you see outside?

MANY COLORS

Nature is full of bright colors. Here are some of the Crayola® colors used in this book.

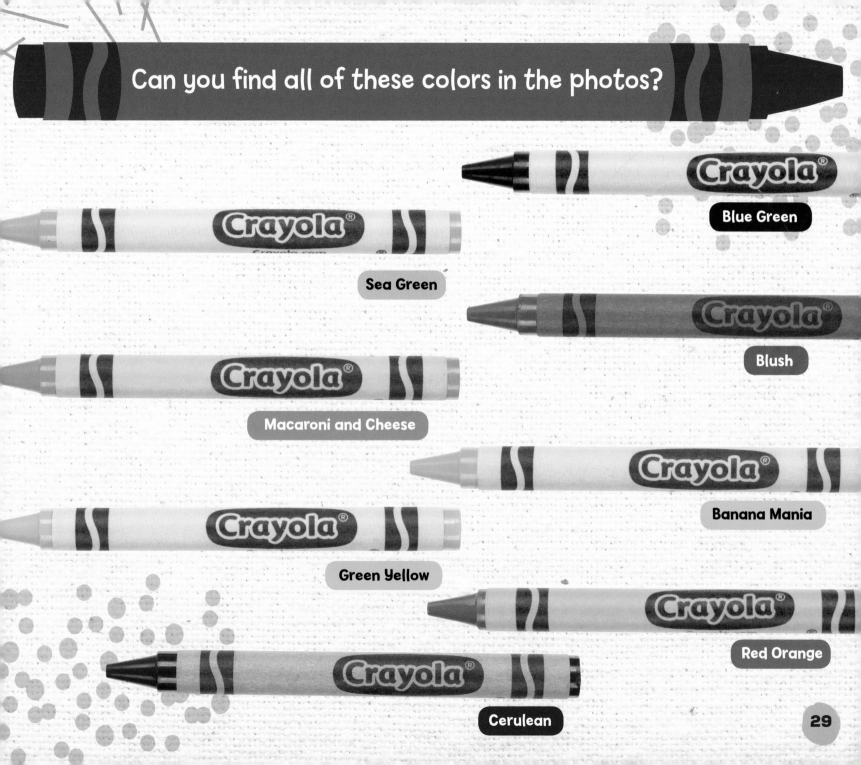

Can you find all of these colors in the photos?

Blue Green

Sea Green

Blush

Macaroni and Cheese

Banana Mania

Green Yellow

Red Orange

Cerulean

GLOSSARY

desert: a dry area with little rain and few plants

grassland: a large, open area covered with grass

nature: everything in the world that isn't made by people. Plants, animals, and the weather are parts of nature.

nectar: a sweet liquid found in many flowers

poison: a substance that can harm or kill

predators: animals that hunt other animals for food

rain forest: a thick forest where a lot of rain falls

TO LEARN MORE

BOOKS

Adamson, Heather. *Purple*. Minneapolis: Jump!, 2014.
Learn about purple plants, animals, and rocks and how colors work in nature.

Borth, Teddy. *Yellow Animals*. Minneapolis: Abdo, 2015.
Read about yellow animals throughout the world and how their color helps them.

Shepherd, Jodie. *Crayola Spring Colors*. Minneapolis: Lerner Publications, 2018.
Explore the wide variety of colors found during the spring season.

WEBSITES

Animal Coloring Pages
http://www.crayola.com/free-coloring-pages/plants-and-animals/animals-coloring-pages/
Visit this website to color several animal coloring pages.

Tree Coloring Pages
http://www.coloring.ws/trees.htm
Visit this website to work on several tree coloring pages.

INDEX

PHOTO ACKNOWLEDGMENTS

The images in this book are used with the permission of: © RoyStudioEU/Shutterstock.com (linen background throughout); Natapong Supalertsophon/Moment/Getty Images, p. 5 (top left); Jorg Greuel/Photonica/Getty Images, p. 5 (top right); iStock.com/Grafner, p. 5 (bottom left); Josemaria Toscano/Shutterstock.com, p. 5 (bottom right); iStock.com/KS-Art, p. 5 (center); iStock.com/Dopeyden, p. 7 (top); iStock.com/Photon-Photos, p. 7 (bottom); UIG Premium/Getty Images, p. 8; iStock.com/FotoSpeedy, p. 9; Kjersti Joergensen/Shutterstock.com, p. 10; iStock.com/numismarty, p. 11; iStock.com/mirceax, p. 13; iStock.com/eli_asenova, p. 15 (top); Adam Gault/OJO Images/Getty Images, p. 15 (bottom); iStock.com/Subaqueosshutterbug, p. 17; Thomas Kitchin & Victoria Hurst/First Light/Getty Images, p. 19; © Hotshotsworldwide/Dreamstime.com, p. 21; Adventure_Photo/E+/Getty Images, p. 23 (top); Tongho58/Moment/Getty Images, p. 23 (bottom); Allan Baxter/DigitalVision/Getty Images, p. 25 (top); Darshan Khanna Photography/Moment/Getty Images, p. 25 (bottom); Vincent Demers Photography/Moment/Getty Images, p. 27; Danita Delimont/Gallo Images/Getty Images, p. 28 (top left); Nikolay Abramov/EyeEm/Getty Images, p. 28 (top right); iStock.com/walkingmoon, p. 28 (bottom left); iStock.com/Adventure_Photo, p. 28 (bottom right); © Tae208/Dreamstime.com, p. 28 (center).

Cover: VarnaK/Shutterstock.com (tulips); Ondrej Prosicky/Shutterstock.com (butterfly); Frozenmost/Shutterstock.com (northern lights); SantiPhotoSS/Shutterstock.com (macaws); RoyStudioEU/Shutterstock.com (linen texture background); TairA/Shutterstock.com (watercolor background).

LERNER e SOURCE

Expand learning beyond the printed book. Download free, complementary educational resources for this book from our website, www.lernerresource.com.